science@work
Communication

MESSENGERS, MORSE CODE, AND MODEMS

By Janice Parker

RSVP
RAINTREE Steck-Vaughn
PUBLISHERS
A Steck-Vaughn Company
Austin, Texas
www.steck-vaughn.com

Published by Raintree Steck-Vaughn, an imprint of Steck-Vaughn Company

Library of Congress Cataloging-in-Publication Data

Parker, Janice.
    Messengers, Morse code, and modems /
  by Janice Parker.
       p.   cm. — (Science [at] work)
    In ser. statement "[at]" appears as the at symbol.
    Includes bibliographical references and index.
    Summary: Discusses the development of various means of communication,
from the printed word through telegraph and telephone to radio, television, and computers,
examining the technology that has made communicating easier.
    ISBN 0-7398-0138-4
    1. Telecommunication—Juvenile literature. [1. Telecommunication. 2. Communication.]
I. Title. II. Series: Science [at] work (Austin, Tex.)
TK5102.4.P35   2000
384--dc21   99-40872
                                      CIP

Printed and bound in Canada
1 2 3 4 5 6 7 8 9 0   04 03 02 01 00

Project Coordinator
Rennay Craats
Content Validator
Lois Edwards
Design
Warren Clark
Copy Editors
Ann Sullivan
Kathy DeVico
Layout and Illustration
Chantelle Sales

Photograph Credits
Every reasonable effort has been made to trace ownership and to obtain permission to reprint copyright material. The publishers would be pleased to have any errors or omissions brought to their attention so that they may be corrected in subsequent printings.

Aero Space Museum Association of Calgary: page 11; **Alexander Graham Bell Association for the Deaf:** page 14; **Corel Corporation:** page 29 top; **Rob Curle:** pages 4 left, 5 bottom left, 17 left, 20 top, 23 bottom, 27 top; **Digital Vision Ltd.:** 43 right; **Eyewire Incorporated:** cover, background pages 2–3, 44–48; pages 3 center, 4 top right, 5 top left, 6 top, 7, 10, 12 top, 16, 17 right, 18, 19, 20 bottom, 22 bottom, 24, 27, 30, 31, 33, 37, 39, 40, 42, 43 left; **Rev. Wilson C. Lee, Ching Chung Taoist Assn. of America:** pages 5 top right, 8; **Pete Malvasi:** pages 3 bottom, 13, 23 top; **Sorcha McGinnis:** pages 5 bottom right, 36; **Michael McPhee:** page 32; **NASA:** pages 21 right, 25; **Regina Leader Post:** pages 3 top, 9; **Telephone Historical Centre, Edmonton, Canada:** page 12 bottom; **TransAlta Utilities:** page 22 top; **Visuals Unlimited:** page 21 left; **Westfile:** page 29 bottom; **George Webber, SAIT:** page 28.

Contents

Have you ever
wondered how books are printed,

or sent a fax,

or used the Internet?

Communication refers to the various ways we send and receive messages. The messages can be in the form of writing, sounds, pictures, or video. Writing letters, publishing newspapers, and broadcasting television programs are just a few of the ways we communicate with each other. Science has developed ways that allow us to communicate more easily and quickly. New jobs are created as new methods of communication are invented. Today contacting other people or receiving current news is as easy as picking up a telephone or turning on a television or a computer. This ease of communication helps us feel closer to people all over the world. New methods of communication, such as satellites and the Internet, have changed the way we interact with one another.

FINDING LINKS

Society

How easily we can communicate has an influence on how we live. Some types of communication can be very useful to us, but they may also affect our health. Some people are concerned that exposure to **radiation** from equipment such as computers will make us sick.

The Environment

Communication makes use of things that are in the environment. Before the invention of paper, people wrote on pieces of tree bark. Inks used for writing and printing were originally made from natural materials.

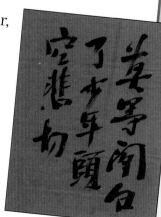

Technology

Communication has changed a great deal over time. Letters were once the best way to communicate with people far away. New inventions such as radios, telephones, televisions, and computers have changed how we communicate and how quickly we can communicate with others.

Careers

There are many careers in the communication field. Publishers create books. Electronic technicians are needed to repair equipment used for communicating. Webmasters maintain computer web pages. As interest in the Internet grows, communication jobs will continue to be in great demand.

Paper

"Don't forget to write."

Long ago, speech and gestures were the only forms of communication. Stories and information were passed by word of mouth. An important change happened when people began to write things down, first on clay, then on **papyrus**, and finally on paper. At first, anything on paper had to be handwritten. Whole books were printed by hand until printing presses were invented.

Typewriters and computers allow us to print our own letters. Even with the many other types of communication, written communication is still very popular. People like to read books, magazines, and newspapers. It has become very easy for publishers to create messages that can be read around the world. People with the right equipment can create their own newspapers and pamphlets at home.

Why is the printed word so important?

Before printing was invented, all books and other **documents** had to be written out by hand. If someone wanted ten copies of the same book, for example, he or she had to write out each of the books. This took a long time. Few people could read, and even fewer people owned books.

Printing, using a machine to place words and pictures on paper, is one form of communicating. Printing allows people to make many copies of the same words or stories. The first printed pages were made in China by carving words and pictures into blocks of wood. The surface of the wood was then covered with ink. The block was pressed down on a piece of paper. By adding more ink to the wood block, many copies of the same words and pictures could be made. The first printed book was made in this way around A.D. 868.

BYTE-SIZED FACT

Typesetting means combining letters to make entire pages of words, or **text**. Today, computers are used for typesetting, so anyone can type and print out letters and other documents.

It was difficult to check text for errors with traditional typesetting machines. As the operator looked at the back of the typesetter, the letters were all backward and clamped into place, ready to be pressed on paper.

Printing Inks

The first inks were used in China and Egypt about 5,000 years ago. They were made of powdered carbon, an element found in all living things. The carbon was mixed with vegetable oil or glue. Much later, water-based inks were made in China. These inks did not contain oil or glue. They were mixed with water. Water-based inks similar to these early inks are still used today.

Hundreds of years ago in Europe, most documents were written on parchment, which was made from stretched sheepskin. Inks made from carbon did not write well on parchment, which was very greasy. Another type of ink was made—iron ink. Iron ink was a mixture of an acid and iron salts from the earth. Iron inks were clear in color, but they slowly darkened to leave marks on parchment.

The first modern inks were invented in the 19th century. Scientists created new dyes in many colors. These dyes were made of natural products added to chemicals.

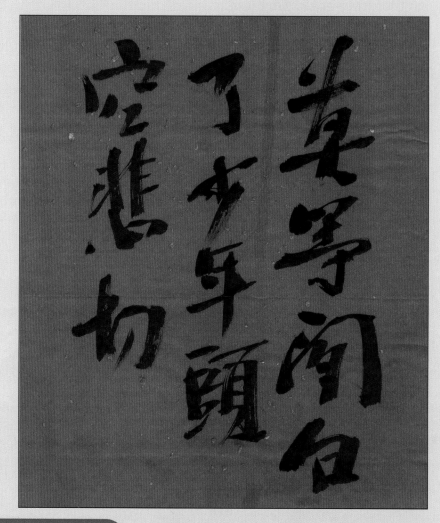

BYTE-SIZED FACT

Many early inks were **toxic** to humans. Inhaling or swallowing these inks was very dangerous. Newer inks, such as those used in books, magazines, and newspapers, do not harm our health.

Calligraphy is the art of making beautiful lettering. It requires a special pen that allows you to vary the thickness of letters. It also uses special ink. Calligraphy has been used in China for hundreds of years.

What does a printing press do?

A printing press is a machine that is used to print many copies of a book or newspaper quickly. It uses ink and special plates to print text and pictures on paper. Johannes Gutenberg invented the first printing press in 1445. His letters, which could be moved around to form different words, were made of metal, and he used an oil-based ink. The letters were placed to form words in a frame, and the words were set in sentences. The letters were then covered in ink. A large piece of paper was placed on top of the inked letters in the frame. The printer then turned a large wood screw to lower a wooden block onto the printing press. This pressed together the letters and the paper. The inked letters were transferred to the paper. More ink and another piece of paper were used to make another copy. This method of printing was sometimes called **letterpress**.

Today many books are printed using a laser typesetter. This printing method uses beams of light to create a photograph or film of the text. Laser beams change the electrical charge of the white areas of the page from positive to negative on a drum, a cylinder in the machine. The area that contains the text and images remains positive. The ink is negatively charged. Positive and negative charges are drawn to each other. As a result, the positive text area attracts the ink. The ink is then transferred on the page or film.

BYTE-SIZED FACT

The Gutenberg press could make about 300 copies a day. Today large printing presses can make thousands of copies in one hour.

Hundreds of rolls of paper are used to make daily newspapers. Fourteen different paper mills supply paper to such newspapers as the *New York Times*.

Publishing

Publishers own and run companies that create books, newspapers, and other types of documents. A publisher finds a writer and illustrator and gathers photographs to create a book or magazine. Once a book is completed, publishers either print it themselves or send it to a printer, who creates many copies that can be sold.

There are many careers in the publishing industry. Writers and illustrators create what will go into a book or magazine. There are often many drafts of the book or article required before it is ready to be published. People who write for newspapers are called journalists.

Editors and proofreaders make sure that the words and grammar are correct. They also make sure that the publication makes sense and that all facts in the book or article are true. Graphic designers are responsible for the overall appearance of the publication, from the cover to the index pages. They create a visual look for a document, deciding what should go where on a page. Designers also put photographs and other images where they look best throughout the book. Photographers take pictures that appear in books, magazines, and newspapers. Production managers make sure the printing process runs smoothly. After it is all finished and printed, marketers and sales people advertise the book or magazine so that people will buy it.

Publishing involves various skills. People with very different strengths can find a rewarding career in publishing.

All the employees at a publisher work closely together to make the best possible product.

How did airplanes change the mail system?

Compared to some forms of communication, delivering letters by mail seems slow to us today. The mail system was once much slower than it is now. At first, people had to travel many miles on foot to deliver a letter. The Pony Express used horses to carry letters.

The first airmail flight took off in 1911. By 1918, airplanes were used regularly to carry mail. You used to have to ask for airmail, but now nearly all mail traveling to other cities is sent by air.

The invention of trains and automobiles sped up mail delivery. Mail could be carried by vehicle to another city, or sometimes to another country. Trains and cars were not very fast, however, so mail took many days to travel from one place to another. When letters were carried by ships across the ocean, it could take many months before they reached their destination.

"Airmail" means sending mail to other areas in the world by airplane. The use of airmail changed the postal system forever. When you use airmail, it takes only hours or a few days for a package or letter to travel across the country or around the world.

Airplanes were invented in the early 1900s and were used to deliver mail several years later. Today mail traveling great distances usually spends some time on an airplane.

BYTE-SIZED FACT
The first airmail flight delivered postcards across India in 1911. Early airmail flights were often difficult for the pilot because there was very little room in the airplane for the mail. The first airmail pilot in the United States carried a bag of letters on his lap as he flew.

Wire

"The line is still busy."

With the invention of the telegraph, people could send information over metal wires or cables. Telephones, telegraphs, and fax machines also use wire communication. They send messages from one electrical machine to another. Communicating by wire means that people can send a message to someone far away without having to wait for a letter to arrive. Wire communication uses electricity to send messages. Scientists discovered how to change letters and sounds into **electrical currents,** or a flow of electricity along a wire. The first communication by wire used a telegraph. Today people can communicate by using telephones and fax machines.

What is a telegraph?

A telegraph is a machine that uses electricity to send messages along wires. The first telegraphs were invented in the early 1800s in Britain and the United States. Before the telegraph, messages had to be written and delivered by mail or by hand.

Telegraph messages are sent by turning electricity on and off. Short bursts of electrical currents are sent along wires to the receiving telegraph. The receiver has magnetic needles on a dial with the letters of the alphabet written on it. Separate wires and coils act as electromagnets and control each needle. The currents from the sending machine cause a magnetic field in the coil. As each letter is sent, the magnetic field makes the needle point to that letter on the dial. This device was later improved to need only two needles.

In 1844 Samuel Morse invented a telegraph that made it even easier and quicker to send messages by telegraph. He developed a code called the Morse Code. Each letter or number is represented by a series of dots and dashes. Dots are created by short bursts of electricity. Dashes are created by longer bursts.

Like all telegraphs, a Morse telegraph is made up of two parts—a sender and a receiver. An operator uses a switch to tap out short or long electrical currents. At the other end, a receiver reads the currents as dots or dashes. The receiver prints the message out on a long piece of paper. The telegraph operator receiving the message then translates the Morse Code back into English.

In 1844 the telegraph was used to announce James K. Polk's nomination for the presidency. After that, newspapers began using Morse's invention to run "telegraph news" from across the country.

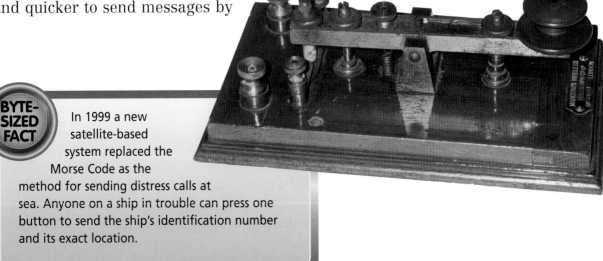

BYTE-SIZED FACT In 1999 a new satellite-based system replaced the Morse Code as the method for sending distress calls at sea. Anyone on a ship in trouble can press one button to send the ship's identification number and its exact location.

How does a telephone work?

Atelephone allows us to communicate with our voices rather than by dots and dashes. Telephones have two parts: a mouthpiece and an earpiece. We speak into the mouthpiece and listen to the earpiece.

The sound waves from your voice are converted into electric current by the transmitter. A carbon transmitter uses a diaphragm, a thin metal disk, and a cup of carbon grains to send signals. The sound waves make the diaphragm vibrate. As it vibrates, it puts pressure on the carbon grains. Electric current flows through the grains. The current copies the pattern of vibrations and sends them to the receiver.

A foil-electret transmitter uses an electrically charged plastic diaphragm with a metal coating on one side. An electric field is created between the diaphragm and a hollow metal disk called a backplate. The vibrations caused by sound waves change the electric field, and the current becomes a copy of the speaker's sound waves.

The receiver, a metal disk in a flexible frame, changes electricity back into sound. It is surrounded by a ring-shaped permanent magnet. Another magnet called an electromagnet is attached to the other side of the diaphragm. When electricity from the sender's message flows through the electromagnet's coil, it becomes magnetized. The magnets pull in different directions and cause vibrations. This creates sound waves that are the same as those sent through the telephone.

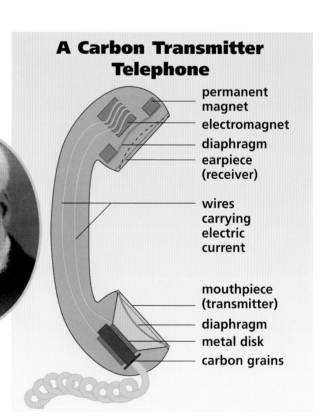

A Carbon Transmitter Telephone

- permanent magnet
- electromagnet
- diaphragm
- earpiece (receiver)
- wires carrying electric current
- mouthpiece (transmitter)
- diaphragm
- metal disk
- carbon grains

BYTE-SIZED FACT

The first telephone was created in 1876. It was made by Alexander Graham Bell. He and his assistant, Watson, made the first long distance phone call in October 1876. They spoke between Boston and Cambridge, Massachusetts. The call covered 2 miles (3.2 km). Now phones reach across the world!

What is a telephone exchange?

Example of Telephone Exchanges

LOCAL CALLS

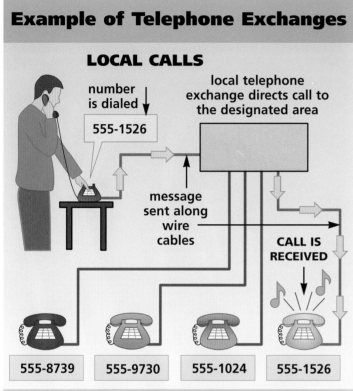

number is dialed

555-1526

local telephone exchange directs call to the designated area

message sent along wire cables

CALL IS RECEIVED

555-8739 555-9730 555-1024 555-1526

INTERNATIONAL CALLS

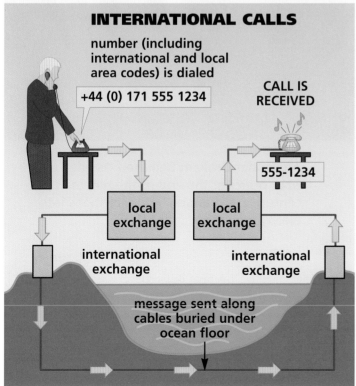

number (including international and local area codes) is dialed

+44 (0) 171 555 1234

CALL IS RECEIVED

555-1234

local exchange local exchange

international exchange international exchange

message sent along cables buried under ocean floor

Telephones use wires or cables to send their messages. Most telephones have a cable that leads to a nearby telephone exchange. These cables can be high up on telephone poles or buried deep underground. When we make a telephone call, our call is connected by cables to the exchange. At the exchange, the call is directed to the area we are calling. When telephones were first invented, people worked at the exchanges and connected the calls by hand. Today exchanges use computers that instantly redirect calls to the correct location.

A local call is simply redirected along another cable. A long-distance call to another country will first be sent by cables or optical fibers to an international exchange. Telephone cables are buried under the ocean floor to connect continents. Radio waves and satellites are also used to send telephone calls.

> We need to use area codes whenever we dial a long-distance number. Area codes connect us to the telephone exchange in the area we are calling.
>
> BYTE-SIZED FACT

What is fiber optics?

In the 1980s scientists found that television cables could carry information better than the copper wires used in telephone lines. They wanted to increase the number of signals that telephone lines and **computer networks** could receive. They turned to fiber optics. Light vibrations are changed into electric pulses, and sound is produced when these pulses vibrate a speaker.

Each fiber has three parts: an inner core of reflective glass or plastic, a middle layer of glass called cladding, and an outside covering of plastic. When light hits the cladding, it reflects back into the core. Light waves travel down the length of a hollow fiber optics cable. Light waves can bend around curves. This makes it possible for one ray of light to travel farther. A device called an encoder measures these waves of light into a series of "on" and "off" pulses. The pulses can be translated into video, computer, or voice data.

A cable may contain one fiber, but there are often dozens of fibers bundled together in the center of the cable. Cables with one fiber carry only one wave of light, so they are faster than cables with many fibers.

Alexander Graham Bell used the idea of fiber optics at the end of the nineteenth century. He changed light vibrations into electric pulses.

BYTE-SIZED FACT

A fiber optic strand is about the same thickness as a single human hair. One strand can carry close to 2,000 telephone calls at one time.

Cellular Telephones

Cellular telephones, also called mobile phones or cell phones, are not connected to telephone exchanges by wires or cables. Cell phones are a combination of a telephone and a two-way radio.

Like most telephones, a cell phone changes voices into electrical currents. Instead of sending the currents along cables, cell phones send waves through the air. These waves are picked up by **antennas** on a receiving and transmitting station.

Receiving and transmitting stations are spread out across an area. Each receives radio signals sent out from a smaller area called a cell. Every cell works on a different **frequency** than its surrounding cells. Cells in one area are all linked to one central computer. If you are moving through an area while using your cell phone, the computer will automatically switch your call to the nearest transmitter.

Some cell phones are tiny but offer many services. These small cell phones weigh under 4 ounces (113 grams). They ring or vibrate and have an answering machine and pager built into them.

BYTE-SIZED FACT

There were 69.2 million cellular telephones in use in the United States alone in 1998.

How can we send pictures over the telephone?

While telephones send voice messages through telephone lines, fax machines send written words and pictures. Fax is short for *facsimile*, which means "copy." Fax machines send an exact copy of what is on a piece of paper through phone lines to another fax machine. This means that handwriting, illustrations, and even photographs can be sent by fax.

Both the sender and the receiver must have a fax machine or a computer with software that enables it to receive faxes. A fax machine divides a page into thousands of tiny squares. Each square is turned into a sound signal that is different depending on the darkness or lightness of the square. When the signals reach the receiving fax machine, they are turned back into squares. The fax machine then prints out a copy of

Fax machines allow people around the world to share documents with each other in seconds. The charge for sending a fax is the same as making a telephone call to the same place.

what the original fax looked like. Sending a fax is as quick as making a phone call.

Some fax machines can make photocopies, scan documents into a computer, or print computer documents. Home fax machines also often have telephone and answering machine features.

BYTE-SIZED FACT
Fax machines were invented in the early 1900s, but they were not commonly used until the 1980s, when they became less expensive.

Electronic Technician

Electronic technicians work to build, install, or repair electrical equipment used for communicating.

Electronic technicians work with equipment such as telephones, televisions, and computer networks. Those who work for telephone companies install and test telephone cables. If telephone systems are not working, the technician repairs the problem. They repair problems at telephone exchanges and repair the cables that connect computers, fax machines, and other electronic equipment.

Advanced technology has created more opportunities for electronic technicians. The popularity of television, telephones, and the Internet means technicians in the communication industry are usually in demand.

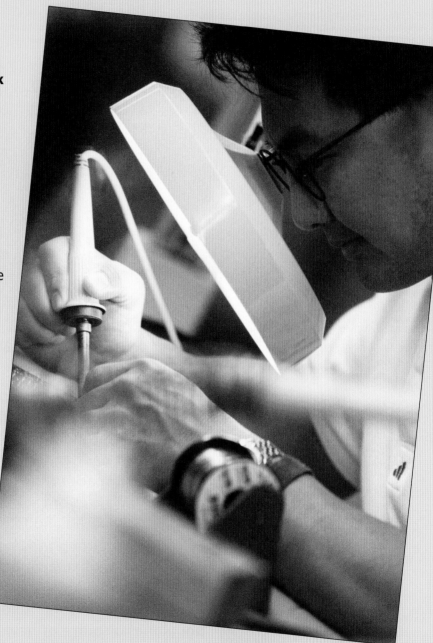

Technical careers can include repairing equipment and operating electronic machinery. Many people working in these positions complete their training in trade schools, technical institutes, or colleges.

Waves

The discovery of electromagnetic waves in the 19th century led to a new form of communication. These waves are created by the movement back and forth of electric charges, and travel through space at the speed of light. Waves do not require wires or cables to send and receive messages. Both radio and television use waves to send messages through the air. Radio became an important form of communication for people, such as sailors, who were not hooked up to telephone cables. Television soon followed, and it became popular as a source of news and entertainment. Wave communication changed a great deal with the first satellites. Satellites allow information to be sent around the world. They make it possible for people to send and receive messages instantly.

What are electromagnetic waves?

Electromagnetic waves allow messages to be sent without using cables or wires. They are electrical and magnetic vibrations that travel through the air. Electromagnetic waves are rays of electrical energy that exist in wave shapes in space. Like waves in water, electromagnetic waves have high points called crests, and low points called troughs. A **wavelength** is the length of a wave from one crest to the next. There are many different types of electromagnetic waves. Ultraviolet rays, which can cause sunburn, are one type. Infrared, Gamma, and X-ray waves are other types. Radio waves, which are used to send messages, have the longest wavelength of all electromagnetic waves. Some radio waves can extend 6,250 miles (10,000 km).

Radio waves can be sent over short distances or even into outer space. Radio signals travel at the speed of light.

Different types of radio waves are used for different purposes. Most radio broadcasts use long or medium-length radio waves. Short-wave radio signals are used for communication across great distances.

The Hubble Space Telescope sends images to a satellite and then down to a receiving center on Earth. Then the signals are sent to another satellite, which bounces them back down to NASA's computer facility.

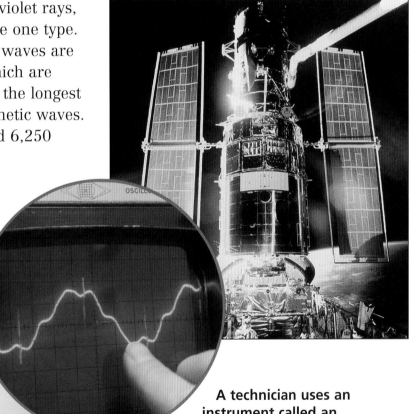

BYTE-SIZED FACT

Electromagnetic waves travel at the speed of light. This is 186,282 miles (299,792 km) per second. The most basic electromagnetic wave is called a plane wave. It moves in a straight line.

A technician uses an instrument called an oscilloscope to look at the shape of electromagnetic waves.

Electromagnetic Fields

Any machines that carry or use electricity, such as telephones, computers, microwave ovens, and power lines, are surrounded by an electromagnetic field (EMF).

Electromagnetic fields (EMFs) are made up of an invisible type of energy that surrounds electrical devices. The closer to the devices, the stronger the field. EMFs are energy that can affect surrounding objects and people. Some researchers who study EMFs believe that EMFs can make humans sick. EMFs do not cause immediate harm. Scientists believe that continued exposure to electromagnetic fields over years may cause cancer in humans.

Other studies have shown no connection between EMFs and human health. To be safe, many scientists believe we should limit our exposure to EMFs. At home or school, this means making sure that you sit at least an arm's length away from electrical appliances such as televisions. Many people believe that you should not use electric blankets, which expose you to EMFs throughout the night.

Some studies suggest that exposure to EMFs from power lines and cell phones causes higher rates of cancer. Others say there is no connection.

Computer monitors release strong EMFs. People who spend several hours a day in front of computers are often told to stay as far away from the screens as possible.

The strongest EMFs are created by large power lines or power plants. Today, city planners try to make sure that there are no homes close to these sources.

What is radio?

Radio is a way to communicate by using electromagnetic waves instead of wires. The waves can carry sounds, such as voices, across long distances. The first radio communication signals were sent by a man named Guglielmo Marconi in 1895. Marconi experimented with radio waves when he was a young man in Italy. He began to send radio waves through the air. Marconi created more powerful telegraph equipment that could send and receive radio signals over longer distances. He was able to send messages in Morse Code over distances of 2 miles (3.2 km). When Marconi moved to England in 1899, he succeeded in sending radio signals across the English Channel.

Early radio telegraph transmitters invented by Marconi led to the development of radio broadcasting as we know it.

BYTE-SIZED FACT

There are two kinds of radio transmissions—amplitude modulation, or AM, and frequency modulation, or FM. AM has lower frequencies than FM. FM has some advantages over AM signals. FM is relatively static-free in thunderstorms and other forms of interference. AM is not. FM also reproduces sound more accurately than AM.

A couple of years later, Marconi sent radio signals from England to Newfoundland, Canada. Other scientists did not think it was possible to send radio waves so far because the Earth is round, and the waves would have to curve around it. Certain types of radio waves can reflect from a layer of the Earth's atmosphere. This allows them to travel around the curve of the Earth.

Soon, radio communication was used by ships at sea. Before radio, ships could only send messages to other ships if they could see one another.

What is two-way radio?

Most radios can only receive signals, not send them. Two-way radio allows people to both send and receive messages. In some areas in the world, there are few or no telephone lines or exchanges. Two-way radio allows people in these areas to talk to one another. It is also used by airplane pilots. The pilots keep in contact with air traffic controllers at airports to find out when it is safe to take off and land. Police, ambulance workers, and firefighters all use two-way radio to stay in contact.

Truck drivers and others use a type of two-way radio, called citizen's band or CB radio, to talk to each other. CB radio allows truckers to warn other drivers of weather or road problems. It is also a way to help pass the time during long trips. CB radio can only be used over very short distances.

Amateur, or ham, radios are another way to communicate. They allow people to pick up and send radio signals around the world. Many people use amateur radios as a hobby. These radios also allow people to communicate during emergencies, when telephone lines are not working.

BYTE-SIZED FACT

People use a special language when speaking by CB radio. "Ten-four" means that they heard and understood the other person's message. "Over" signals the other person to reply, and "out" means no reply is necessary and the conversation has finished.

Many truck drivers use a CB radio to communicate. These radios keep them company on their trips. Many people have special nicknames that they use on the air.

Satellites

It is sometimes difficult to send radio signals over long distances. The waves can have problems traveling over hills and mountains. The round shape of the Earth also makes it difficult to send waves. To travel around the curve of Earth, waves have to bounce off the ionosphere, a layer in the sky that reflects waves back down to Earth. Communication satellites, sometimes called comsats, make it easy to send signals around the world.

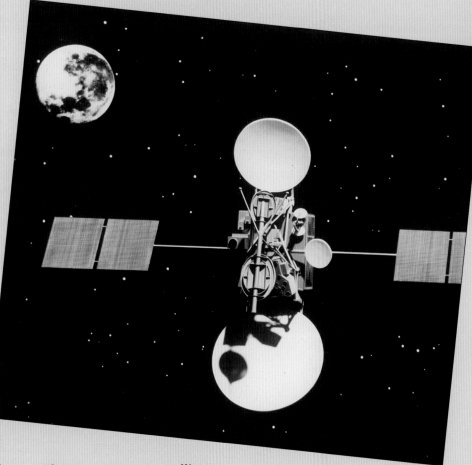

A satellite is an instrument that orbits Earth. Communication satellites pick up radio waves transmitted from Earth and bounce them back to other locations on Earth.

The first communication satellite was sent into space in 1960. This satellite, called *Echo I*, was shaped like a huge metal ball. It reflected weak microwave signals back to Earth. A more powerful communication satellite, *Telstar*, was sent into orbit in 1962. *Telstar* worked very well and communicated with

There are many satellites in orbit at the same time. Sometimes radio waves from one satellite interfere with those from another satellite.

transmitting and receiving stations in the United States and Great Britain.

BYTE-SIZED FACT

Most long-distance telephone calls use a system of satellites called *Intelsat*. Intelsat stands for International Telecommunications Satellite Organization. It has about 15 satellites in orbit around Earth.

How does television work?

Television is similar to radio, but it uses pictures as well as sounds to communicate. Television turns sound and pictures into electrical signals. These signals are sent into the air as radio waves. A receiver in your television turns the signals back into sound and pictures.

A television signal starts when light from the scene being filmed enters the camera. The camera changes the light into electric signals. A microphone picks up the sound and changes those waves into electric signals at the same time. These signals are then sent to the television receiver. The receiver makes sense of the signals and then changes them back into copies of the light and sound waves recorded by the camera. This is what we see on our television screens.

The first televisions were very large with small screens. When television was invented, there was only one channel to watch, and it only broadcast for a few hours a day. Only black-and-white images were available. Color television began in the 1960s. Color television signals are broken down into red, green, and blue light. These signals are changed back to the original colors in our television sets.

BYTE-SIZED FACT
Television screens, whatever their size, all have the same ratio of width to height. All television screens are 4 units wide by 3 units high.

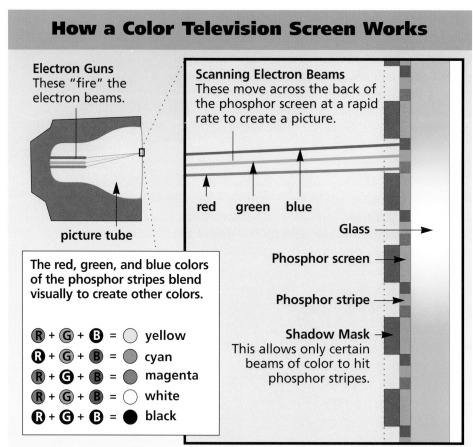

How a Color Television Screen Works

Electron Guns
These "fire" the electron beams.

picture tube

Scanning Electron Beams
These move across the back of the phosphor screen at a rapid rate to create a picture.

red   green   blue

Glass

Phosphor screen

Phosphor stripe

Shadow Mask
This allows only certain beams of color to hit phosphor stripes.

The red, green, and blue colors of the phosphor stripes blend visually to create other colors.

R + G + B = yellow
R + G + B = cyan
R + G + B = magenta
R + G + B = white
R + G + B = black

What are cable television and satellite television?

Television sets need antennas to receive television signals from local stations. Some homes and other buildings have television antennas on their roofs to pick up the signals. These antennas must be close to a local television station in order to pick up the signals. Cable television and satellite television allow us to receive signals from much farther away.

To get cable television, you must go through a cable company. At first, cable television signals were sent through wires, or cables, that connect the cable television company to your home. Today cable television companies also use communications satellites to transmit signals. If you have your own **satellite dish**, you can get television signals from around the world without using a cable

company. A satellite dish is a special type of antenna that receives signals directly from satellites in space. While you may only have access to a few local channels, there are hundreds of cable channels. There are even more channels available by satellite.

Television antennas must be as high above the ground as possible. They are often placed on rooftops so signals can be easily received.

How do television cameras and video cameras work?

A television camera takes pictures and turns each picture into hundreds of lines. The camera scans each line electronically to figure out how bright it is and which colors it contains. Television cameras contain three tubes to pick up all the colors in an image. The tubes create signals that differ depending on the color. Because television images move, the camera scans these lines 25 to 30 times per second. The images are sent, line by line, as electrical signals to a receiver.

Video cameras work the same way as television cameras, but they are less powerful and do not reproduce images as clearly. Video cameras use **microchips**, tiny metal disks that contain the electrical circuitry needed to run computers, instead of tubes to record images. Camcorders are small, handheld video cameras. Sound is recorded by a small microphone on the camcorder.

Video cameras can store images on videotape or video disks. When a videotape is played back, the moving tape produces electrical signals that are turned back into images. Underneath its smooth surface, a compact disk has another layer that is made up of higher and lower areas. Video disks use a laser beam to read these high and low points on the disk. Video disks last longer than videotapes. The magnetic tape in videotapes is more easily damaged than a videodisk.

BYTE-SIZED FACT The word *video* means "to see." Video recorders were invented soon after the television.

Television camera operators film people and events for television programs. Their footage can be transmitted to the television station immediately and broadcast over the air live.

Noise Pollution

When we think of pollution, we usually think of problems that affect the land and air, such as garbage or smog caused by automobiles. However, there are some kinds of pollution, such as noise pollution, that cannot be seen.

Noise pollution can be annoying. It is very difficult to work or sleep if you are surrounded by loud noise. Noise pollution can also be dangerous. Very loud noises can cause hearing loss. Even quieter noises can damage our eardrums if we listen to them long enough.

Both radios and televisions are designed to make very loud sounds. Many people wear headsets, which are earphones attached to a headband, to listen to radios or television. Headsets allow us to listen without bothering the people around us, but listening to loud music or television through a headset can also damage our hearing.

Traffic and construction areas are noise polluters. Many people working in construction wear earphones to protect their hearing.

Sounds are measured in decibels. A whisper is about 30 decibels, while normal conversation is about 60 decibels. A jackhammer is 130 decibels. Long exposure to any noise above 90 decibels, such as a lawn mower can cause hearing loss. Most governments have made laws to protect people from noise pollution. Such laws may not allow sound over a certain level during the night, so people can sleep. They also may not allow loud noises in neighborhoods where many people live.

Computers

"We need to set up a computer link."

Computers have changed the way people communicate. Through digital information and computer networks, people are able to communicate quickly and inexpensively. The Internet has had a huge impact all over the world. It allows people to find information on almost any subject. People can also use the Internet and electronic mail to send messages around the world. While some other forms of communication are expensive or difficult to use, nearly anyone can use the Internet. Millions of people now use this system, and millions more will soon be connected.

How are sounds and pictures digitized?

Computers have led to a new communication technology called digitization. Digitization means changing pieces of information, such as sounds and images, into digital information. Digital information is all of the same information carried by electrical signals changed into **binary code**. Binary code is the system that is used to run all computers and electronics. Binary numbers are a series of the numbers 0 and 1. In the binary system, an electrical current is either on (1) or off (0).

Binary numbers can be put together in different combinations called binary codes. Binary codes can represent numbers, letters, pictures, and sounds. Digitized information has much better sound and picture quality than other systems, such as radio waves. Also, many digital signals can be sent along a single wire at the same time. Computers easily store and send digital information. Computers store information on their hard drive. They send information through a network or over a **modem**.

In a binary system, zeros and ones are placed in different orders to represent different characters and numbers.

BYTE-SIZED FACT

Digital television is becoming increasingly popular. It converts sounds and images electronically into binary code. Digital television transmitters do not need to send the information contained in every picture frame. Only the changes from frame to frame are sent. This means that the information can be sent more quickly, and that more than one signal can be sent over a single cable. Digital television will allow us to have access to even more television stations than ever.

How do computers talk to one another?

In order for us to communicate using computers, the machines must be able to talk to one another. A computer network is a connection between two or more computers. It allows digital information to be sent quickly from one computer to many other computers. Through a network, a computer can send messages to other computers almost anywhere in the world.

There are two types of computer networks: Local Area Networks (LANs) and Wide Area Networks (WANs). Computers in one office or building can be connected by wires or optical fibers, thin glass wires that transmit information at the speed of light, in a LAN.

Computers in different buildings or even different countries are linked into a WAN by telephone lines. This is done using a device called a modem, which changes computer information into signals that can travel along telephone lines. Modems change digital information into electrical signals. These signals are transferred over telephone lines to other modems connected to computers.

BYTE-SIZED FACT
Modem speed is measured in **bits**, or tiny pieces of information, per second. Fast modems can send thousands of words and other information in a few seconds.

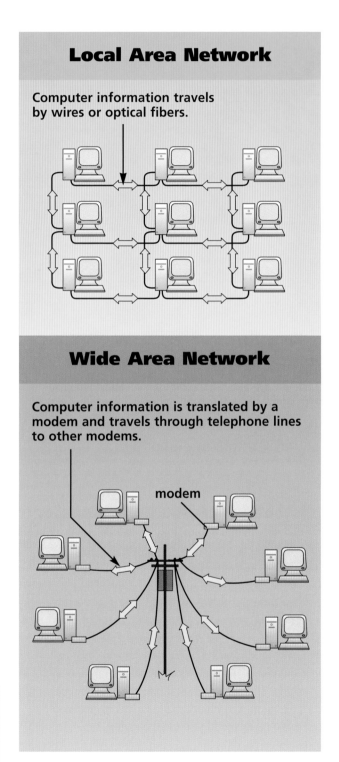

Local Area Network

Computer information travels by wires or optical fibers.

Wide Area Network

Computer information is translated by a modem and travels through telephone lines to other modems.

modem

Video Conference

Computers and video cameras can work together to allow people in different locations to talk face-to-face with each other.

During a video conference, a small video camera sits on top of a computer monitor and is connected to the computer. While people in the room watch the computer, the video camera takes pictures of them. Their image is sent to the other meeting location. In this way, people in different offices can see and talk with one another. A businessperson can meet with people across the country without leaving the office.

In the near future, we may all be using videophones instead of regular telephones. Videophones allow us to have small video conferences. The phones are attached to a small video screen that lets us see the person we have called.

Video conferences allow people to do business with people in other cities or countries. They can meet face-to-face through a computer.

Interactive television may soon become available. It would allow us to send messages to people in the programs we watch. We could also take part in quiz shows or order products directly from our television.

BYTE-SIZED FACT

What is the Internet?

The Internet, sometimes called the Net, is the largest computer network in the world. People around the world are connected to it through their computers. The Internet is like a large network made up of many smaller networks. Anyone with access to a computer, a modem, and a telephone can use the Internet.

The Internet began in 1969. At first it was used only by the United States military. Soon it was also used to send mail electronically. Governments, universities, and businesses began to exchange messages and information over the Internet. Most people did not use the Internet at first because few people had a

computer at home. In the 1980s, the development of small, inexpensive personal computers (PCs) meant that more people could afford a computer. They could also hook up to the Internet.

The Internet allows people to send messages around the world quickly and cheaply. We can also use the Internet to find information on almost any topic.

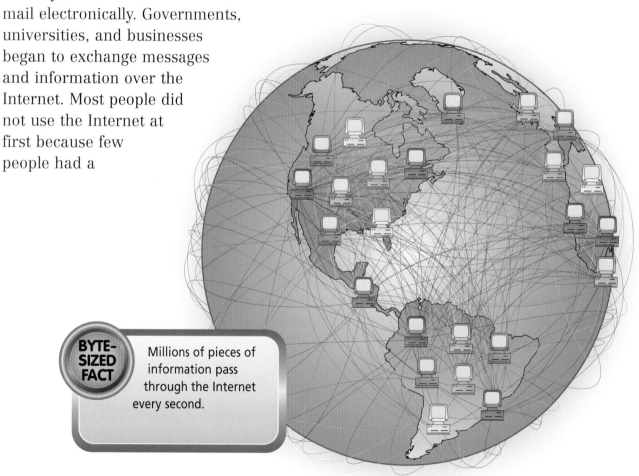

BYTE-SIZED FACT
Millions of pieces of information pass through the Internet every second.

How is the World Wide Web different from the Internet?

The Internet is a worldwide network of computers. It connects millions of users through computers and phone lines. The World Wide Web is mostly used on the Internet. It is a way to find information on the Internet.

The Web is made up of millions of web pages. Web pages contain information in many forms, including words, pictures, sounds, and even video. The Web uses **hyperlinks** to travel from one web page to another. Hyperlinks are either pictures or underlined words that are connected to other sites or documents on the Web. Underlined words are called hypertext. When you click on a hyperlink, you are taken to a different web page. Along with electronic mail (e-mail), the Web is the most popular part of the Internet.

The World Wide Web is very easy to use if you have an Internet connection and a **browser**. A browser is a computer program that helps people move around the Web. **Search engines**, programs that help people find specific web pages, allow people to search for web pages on certain subjects. More and more businesses and people have developed their own websites.

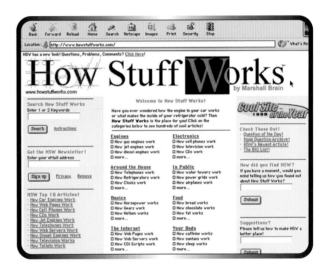

Web pages used to be mainly text. Now pages have sophisticated graphics to draw Internet surfers into the site.

Anatomy of a Website Address

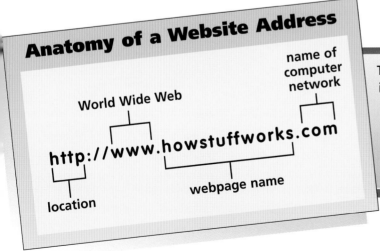

The World Wide Web was created in 1989 in Switzerland. The first web browsers could only view words, not pictures. The first **graphical** web browser appeared in 1993.

BYTE-SIZED FACT

Webmasters and Web Designers

The World Wide Web is made up of millions of web pages.

Most companies have websites to attract new business. They often hire web designers to make those sites stand out.

Web designers and developers create web pages for companies or for individual people. The web developer makes sure the website includes all the information and other features, such as photos and video, that the company wants to let the public know about.

Webmasters are the people who maintain web pages. Large companies often hire a full-time webmaster. The webmaster makes sure the website is running smoothly. All of the information must be up-to-date, so the webmaster makes changes to the site when necessary.

He or she must also make sure that all e-mail sent to the website is answered. Smaller companies may hire a part-time webmaster to keep their site current.

BYTE-SIZED FACT

New computer programs make it easy for anyone to design a personal web page. The programs allow you to put words, pictures, and sound on your page.

What are newsgroups?

Most people using electronic mail send messages to just one person at a time. Sometimes people prefer to use the Internet to speak to groups of people. Newsgroups are groups of a few, or a few hundred, computer users who talk to each other through the Internet. There are newsgroups for many subjects, including television shows, weather, and sports. Newsgroups are a part of the Internet called Usenet.

Newsgroups allow people to discuss issues that interest them. All they need is a computer and the Internet.

Newsgroups can be unmoderated, which means anyone can post information that they want the group to read. Newsgroups can also be moderated, which means that all messages are sent to someone who reads them first and only posts what he or she feels is appropriate. Some groups have mailing lists. Any new postings are automatically e-mailed to the people on the list. Other groups wait until several people have sent messages. Then they send a collection of new messages with an index so members know what kind of information is included in the messages.

Anyone can read the letters that have been sent to a newsgroup. People using a newsgroup do not need to send a message in order to read other messages in the newsgroup.

BYTE-SIZED FACT

Newsgroups discuss a single topic. But there is a newsgroup on the Internet for nearly any topic you could imagine. Even if you were not contributing to a newsgroup discussion, they are great places to find information about a topic.

Electronic Mail

Electronic mail, or e-mail, is a way of sending messages over the Internet. E-mail is the fastest way to send a written letter. Once a message is typed out and sent, it takes only seconds to reach another computer anywhere in the world.

Before e-mail, it was not as easy to send messages to people who lived far away. Long-distance telephone calls can be expensive. Letters sent by mail are cheaper, but they can take many days to travel to other countries, even by airmail. E-mail is both quick and inexpensive. You can e-mail someone in another country and receive an answer from them right away.

When you send an e-mail message, your computer directs it to a computer called a mail server. That computer then sends your message to the proper e-mail address. Your

letter gets stored in the receiver's electronic mailbox until he or she opens it. This process can take seconds, even if the message is being sent across the world.

Getting an e-mail address is simple. Users can sign up for e-mail with an **Internet service provider**. You create a user name and password, which

allows you to access your mailbox and send messages. This is called an e-mail account. Even people who do not own computers can use e-mail. Accounts can be set up for free on the Internet. Many groups and libraries allow people to use computers to send and receive e-mail. E-mail helps people communicate quickly and easily with friends and relatives. It can be used to send more than simple letters. With proper equipment and software, pictures, sounds, video clips, and even computer programs can be sent via the Internet.

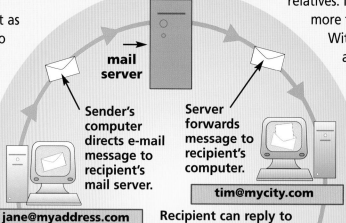

mail server

Sender's computer directs e-mail message to recipient's mail server.

Server forwards message to recipient's computer.

jane@myaddress.com

tim@mycity.com

Recipient can reply to the sender or forward the sent message to other recipients.

mail server

Anatomy of an E-mail Address

mikesmith@myaddress.com

recipient's e-mail name | "at" | domain (or location) where the recipient has his or her mailbox

POINTS OF VIEW

Should the Government Control What Is on the Web?

The Internet continues to grow each year. More people are connected, and new web pages are added. Much of what is on the Internet is useful information, but there are many web pages that are considered inappropriate, especially for children. Hate groups, organizations that are hostile toward certain groups of people, have websites. Some sites focus on adult entertainment. Other web pages discuss topics that may be illegal. It is easy to find these websites, even by accident.

Some people believe that the government or an international group should limit the type of information on the Internet. They believe it is necessary to protect people who use the Internet from encountering bad web pages. They also believe it should be illegal to have websites that contain illegal information.

Other people do not think the government has the right to **censor** what is on the Internet. The Net has become a place where people are free to say or show whatever they want. Trying to control the information would be nearly impossible because thousands of web pages are added to the Internet each day.

"The Internet has a great deal of information and entertainment to offer, but it should not be a refuge for behavior deemed unacceptable in society. Citizens with a government of, by, and for the people are reasonable to expect laws regarding conduct in cyberspace that are consistent with laws in the real world." **U.S. journalist**

"What I do have a problem with is the larger providers that are in between everybody [and] that decide on their own to start filtering and blocking people out. I've got clients that couldn't get from point A to point B because somewhere in the middle there was one of the larger providers filtering." **Employee of a large computer company**

"The Internet is global; it is huge; it needs to broken down and censored. We are breaking it down into a safe place for children." **Canadian Internet provider**

"The government should not have the right to censorship. Censorship is the repression of freedom of speech and expression." **Internet user**

What other points of view might there be on this issue?
What do you think?

Science Survey

How often do you use the different types of machines discussed in this book? We all use telephones. Most of us also have televisions at home and use computers at home or at school. You may not realize just how often you use these communication tools.

What are your answers?

1. How many times do you use a telephone every day? Every week?
2. How many telephones do you have in your home? Does anyone in your family have a cellular telephone?
3. Is there more than one television set in your home? How many are there?
4. How many hours of television do you watch every day? Every week?
5. Do you have a computer? How often do you use it?
6. How many hours a week do you spend using the Internet at home and at school?

Survey Results

There are 120 million telephones in the United States, more than in any other country. Canadians have 16 million telephones.

According to Reading Across America, an organization that offers programs that encourage young people to read, the average young person spends 30 hours a week watching TV or playing video games. By the time a child graduates from high school, he or she will have spent 20,000 hours in front of a television and only 13,000 in a classroom. The average American watches almost 50 hours of television a week.

Four out of 10 homes in the United States have a computer. One-third of these have a modem. Almost 20 percent of all households in the United States have access to the Internet.

Here is your challenge:

For one week, keep track of how often you use the telephone and how much time you spend watching television or using a computer.

On a piece of paper, make three columns. In one column put a checkmark for each time you answer the telephone or make a telephone call. In the second column, write down how many hours you spend watching television each day. In the third, write down how many hours you spend on the computer.

At the end of the week, add up the checkmarks and hours to see how often you use these methods of communication.

Fast Facts

1. Before trains and automobiles were invented, urgent messages were delivered by men on horseback.

2. The first printing press was similar to the presses used to make cider and olive oil.

3. In Morse Code, the letters SOS are used to say that the sender of the message is in trouble. SOS was chosen because the letters were easy to remember: three dots stand for the letter S, and three dashes for the letter O.

4. In 1866 a telegraph cable was laid beneath the Atlantic Ocean. For the first time, telegrams could be sent from England to North America.

5. The more words a telegram contains, the more it costs to send. People sending telegrams keep their messages short.

6. Portable, or cordless, telephones are different from cellular telephones. The receiver of a portable phone communicates with the base of the phone through radio waves. The base of the phone is connected by telephone lines.

7. Fiber-optic cables are as thin as human hairs, but they can transmit thousands of telephone calls at a time.

8. Answering machines answer our phones and record messages from the callers. There are also phones that tell you the number of the person calling as soon as the phone rings.

9. The first radios were very large and heavy. After small electronic devices that control electric current called transistors were invented, portable radios became popular.

10. The smallest television in the world is about the size of a wristwatch.

11. Closed-circuit televisions, a television system that sends images by cable to linked television sets are used by security officers to see what is happening in a building. Videotapes from these cameras can be used to catch criminals.

12. Space shuttles take satellites into space. Astronauts on space shuttle missions can capture and repair satellites in space.

13. Radio signals allow us to communicate with astronauts in space. Television images can also be beamed between Earth and a space shuttle.

14. Communication satellites travel in an orbit 22,000 miles (35,400 km) above the Earth.

15. Laser beams are used to create holograms, a type of three-dimensional photograph. Some day, holograms might be used to make 3-D television and movies.

16. Every web page on the Internet has its own address, called an URL, or Universal Resource Locator.

17. Web pages on the Internet are written in a special type of computer language called HTML, which stands for HyperText Markup Language.

18. Computer viruses are small programs designed to destroy computer systems. They can be transmitted through the Internet.

19. People called hackers use the Internet to break into computer systems for private information.

20. By 2005, as many as 500 million people will be using the Internet around the world.

Experiment on your own with science used in communication.

Make a simple printing press.

What You Need:
A rubber eraser
A knife to cut the eraser
Two flat pieces of wood or stiff cardboard
Glue
Ink
Paper

What to Do:
Ask an adult to help you cut the eraser into long, thin strips. Glue the strips on one of the boards to shape a word or words. **Note: The words and letters must all be backward**. Carefully use a small paintbrush or ink pad to apply ink to the eraser letters pasted on the first board. Place the paper over your words. Place the second board over the paper. Press down evenly on the top board for several seconds. Remove the top board, and then carefully remove the paper. Your words should now be printed on the paper.

eraser strips glued onto board

Create your own radio waves.

What You Need:
A flashlight battery
A radio
A long piece of wire

What to Do:
Turn the radio on. Hold or tape one end of the wire against one end of the battery. Place the middle of the wire very close to the radio. Touch the other end of the wire against the other end of the battery. The power of the battery should create radio waves in the wire. You will be able to hear the waves as crackling sounds of static on the radio.

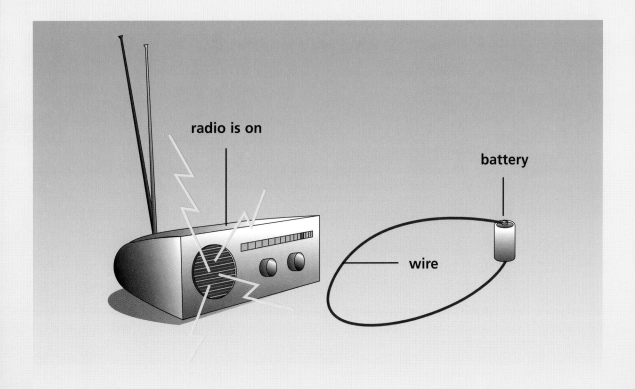

radio is on

battery

wire

Research on Your Own

There are many places to learn about communication. Your school, local library, and the Internet all have excellent resources for you. Here are some to try.

Great Books

Jennings, Terry. *Communication (Making Science Work).* Austin, Texas: Raintree Steck-Vaughn, 1996.

Kerrod, Robin. *Communications (Let's Investigate Science).* New York: Marshall Cavendish, 1994.

Oxlade, Chris. *Electronic Communication.* New York: Franklin Watts, 1997.

Oxlade, Chris. *Telecommunications (20th Century Inventions).* Austin, Texas: Steck-Vaughn, 1997.

Snedden, Robert. *The Internet (20th Century Inventions.)* Austin, Texas: Raintree Steck-Vaughn, 1998.

Great Websites

Eyes in the Skies—Artificial Satellites for the Beginner
www.li.net/~stmarya/phys97/home.htm

Pasadena Kid's Page—Alexander Graham Bell Links
www.e-znet.com/kids/AlexBellLinks.html

Surfing the Net with Kids
www.surfnetkids.com

Glossary

antenna: A device that sends and receives radio signals. Antennas can be shaped like a metal wire or a dish.

binary code: A system that breaks down information and stores it as combinations of the numbers 0 and 1

bits: The smallest piece of information available to computers. It is either a 0 or a 1. All digital information is stored as bits.

browser: A computer program that allows us access to the World Wide Web

censor: To decide that something will not be made available to the public

computer network: Two or more computers linked by wires or telephone lines

document: Anything that is made up of written words

electrical currents: The flow of electricity along wires

frequency: The number of times an electric wave vibrates each second

graphical: Something that contains images such as photographs, drawings, charts, or diagrams

hyperlink: Pictures or words on the World Wide Web that connect you to another web page with the click of a mouse

interactive: A machine that allows us to send and receive messages

Internet service provider: A company that has large computers hooked into the Internet. Home and business users must connect to a service provider in order to have access to the Net.

letterpress: A type of printing in which paper and inked words in a frame are pressed together

microchips: Small machines, which are smaller than your fingernail, that make computers and other electronic devices work

modem: A machine that changes computer information into signals that can travel along telephone lines

papyrus: An ancient writing material made from plants

radiation: High-energy particles or rays that can cause damage to living tissue

satellite dish: A special antenna that can pick up radio waves reflected from satellites in space

search engine: Programs on the World Wide Web that help people find certain web pages

text: Written words or letters

toxic: Dangerous to human health or the environment

wavelength: The distance between two points on a moving wave

Index

airmail 11, 38
antennas 17, 27, 47

binary code 31, 47
bits 32, 47
browser 35, 47

cable television 27
cellular telephone 5, 17, 22, 41, 42
computer 4, 5, 6, 15, 16, 17, 18, 19, 21, 22, 28, 30, 31, 32, 33, 34, 35, 36, 37, 38, 39, 40, 41, 43, 47
computer network 16, 19, 30, 31, 32, 34, 35, 47

digital information 30, 31, 32, 47

electrical currents 12, 13, 17, 31, 47
electromagnetic fields 22
electromagnetic waves 20, 21, 23
electronic mail 30, 35, 37, 38

fax machines 12, 18, 19
fiber optics 16, 42
frequency 17, 23, 47

graphical 35, 47

hyperlink 35, 47

ink 5, 7, 8, 9, 44
Internet 4, 5, 19, 30, 34, 35, 37, 38, 39, 41, 43, 46, 47

letterpress 9, 47

microchip 28, 47
modem 31, 32, 34, 41, 47
Morse Code 13, 23, 42

newsgroups 37
noise pollution 29

papyrus 6, 47
permanent magnet 14
printing press 6, 9, 42, 44
publisher 5, 6, 10

radiation 5, 47
radio 5, 17, 20, 21, 23, 24, 26, 29, 43, 45, 47
radio waves 15, 21, 23, 25, 26, 31, 42, 45, 47

satellite 4, 13, 15, 20, 21, 25, 27, 43, 46
satellite dish 27, 47
search engine 35, 47

telegraph 12, 13, 23, 42
telephone 4, 5, 12, 14, 15, 16, 17, 18, 19, 20, 22, 24, 25, 32, 33, 34, 38, 40, 41, 42, 47
telephone exchange 15, 17, 24
television 4, 5, 16, 19, 20, 22, 26, 27, 28, 29, 31, 33, 37, 40, 41, 43
television camera 28
two-way radio 24

video 4, 16, 28, 33, 35, 36, 38, 41, 43
video camera 28, 33

wavelength 21, 47
webmaster 5, 36
World Wide Web 35, 36, 39, 46, 47